Piano Solo

A JAZZ PIANO
CHRISTMAS

ISBN 978-1-4803-4439-6

HAL•LEONARD®
CORPORATION

7777 W. BLUEMOUND RD. P.O. BOX 13819 MILWAUKEE, WI 53213

Visit Hal Leonard Online at

BALULALOW

Written by PETER WARLOCK
Pseudonym of PHILIP ARNOLD HESELTINE

Moderately, somewhat freely

mp

With pedal

CHRISTMAS HYMN

Words and Music by
BILLY CHILDS

Moderately slow, in 2; somewhat freely

with pedal

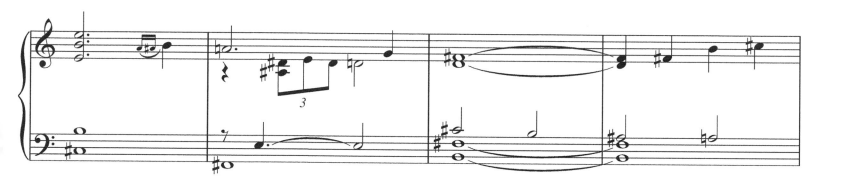

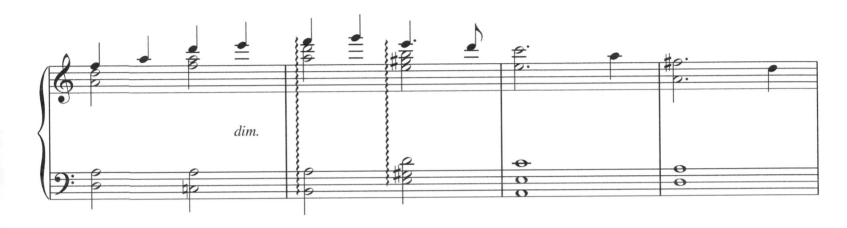

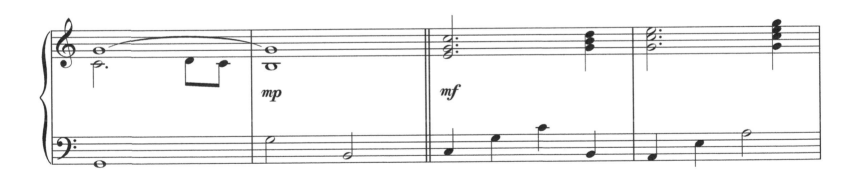

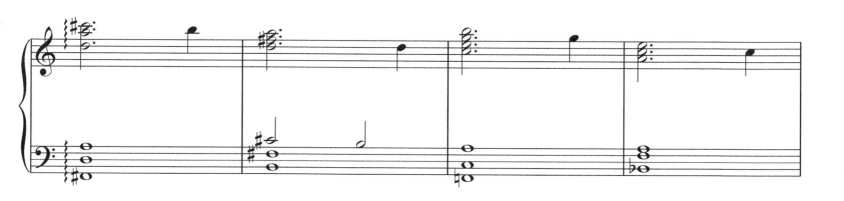

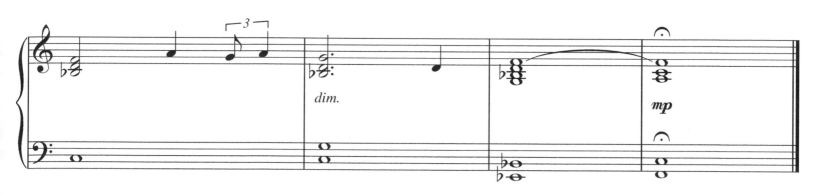

A CHILD IS BORN

By THAD JONES

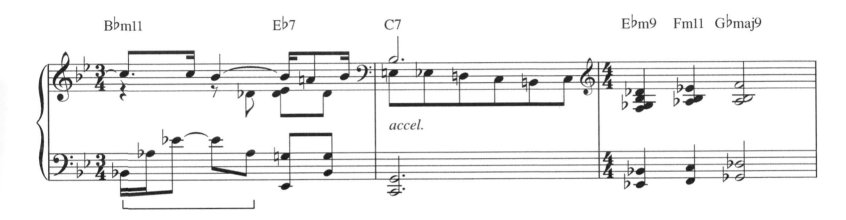

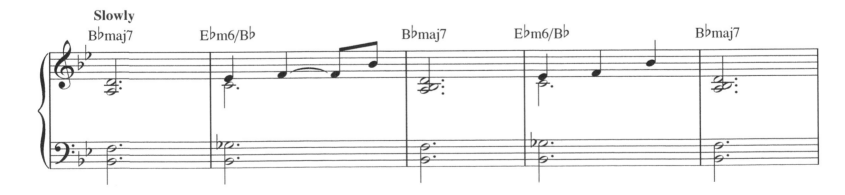

THE CHRISTMAS SONG
(Chestnuts Roasting on an Open Fire)

Music and Lyric by MEL TORMÉ
and ROBERT WELLS

CHRISTMAS TIME IS HERE
from A CHARLIE BROWN CHRISTMAS

Words by LEE MENDELSON
Music by VINCE GUARALDI

HAVE YOURSELF
A MERRY LITTLE CHRISTMAS

from MEET ME IN ST. LOUIS

Words and Music by HUGH MARTIN
and RALPH BLANE

Moderately slow, in 2

No Swing (♪♫ = ♪♫)

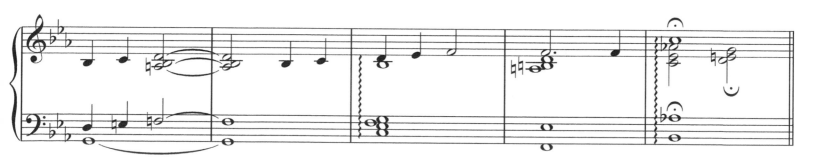

Tempo I

I'LL BE HOME FOR CHRISTMAS

Words and Music by KIM GANNON
and WALTER KENT

I SAW MOMMY KISSING SANTA CLAUS

Words and Music by
TOMMIE CONNOR

Moderately slow ($\sqcap\sqcap = \sqcap^3$)

Double time (still swung)

Half time (still swung)

MY FAVORITE THINGS

from THE SOUND OF MUSIC

Lyrics by OSCAR HAMMERSTEIN II
Music by RICHARD RODGERS

Moderately slow, in 1

SANTA CLAUS IS COMIN' TO TOWN

Words by HAVEN GILLESPIE
Music by J. FRED COOTS

SLEIGH RIDE

By LEROY ANDERSON

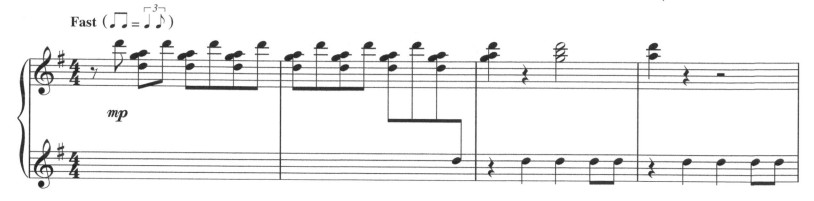

Tempo I

SOME CHILDREN SEE HIM

Lyric by WIHLA HUTSON
Music by ALFRED BURT

Moderately fast, freely

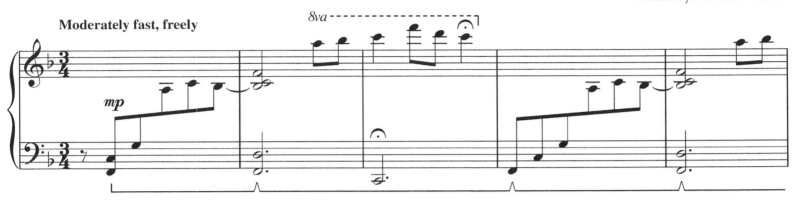

WINTER WONDERLAND

Words by DICK SMITH
Music by FELIX BERNARD

Moderately

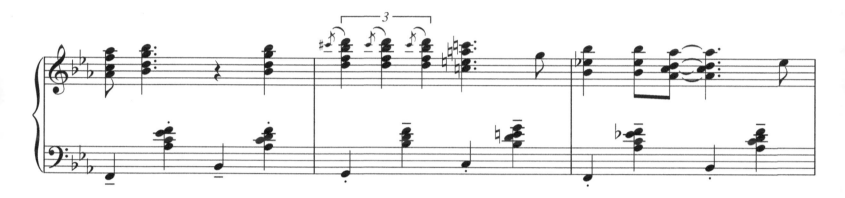